PEOPLE OF THE BOOK

PEOPLE

Edited and Designed by
DAVE FOSTER

With Contribution by
TEDDY KOLLEK
Mayor of Jerusalem

Collins

OF THE BOOK

An Artistic Exploration
of the Bible by

Jossi Stern

PEOPLE OF THE BOOK
Portrayed by Jossi Stern
Editing & Design by Dave Foster
Production and co-edition by Angus Hudson

Copyright © 1979
Interskrift Förlags AB, Herrljunga, Sweden

First printing 1979

Bible quotations from THE LIVING BIBLE
Copyright © 1971 by Tyndale House Publishers, Wheaton, Illinois 60187.
All rights reserved.

Australia, by Collins, Sydney
Canada, by Collins, Toronto
France, by Editions Farel, Paris
Germany, by Brunnen Verlag, Giessen
Holland, by Gideon, Hoornaar
Israel (English Language), by Steimatzky, Jerusalem, Tel-Aviv
New Zealand, by Collins, Auckland
Norway, by Luther Forlag, Oslo
South Africa, by Collins, Johannesburg
Sweden, by InterSkrift, Herrljunga
Switzerland, by Brunnen Verlag, Basle
United Kingdom, by Collins, London and Glasgow
United States, by Collins, Cleveland, Ohio

First published in Great Britain 1979 U.K. ISBN 0 00 513001-08
First published in U.S.A. 1979 U.S.A. ISBN 0-529-05639-9
Library Congress Catalogue Number 78-19574

Printed in Great Britain by Purnell & Sons Ltd., Paulton

CONTENTS

7   INTRODUCTION
    by Dave Foster

9   PREFACE
    by Jossi Stern

13 THE PROMISE

16 THE FIRST FAMILY

30 THE TWELVE TRIBES

35 A MAN NAMED MOSES

56 A KING CALLED DAVID

72 PROPHETS AND KINGS

98 DRY BONES RISE AGAIN

113 CITY OF THE BOOK
    by Teddy Kollek

123 BIOGRAPHICAL NOTES

124 INDEX OF BIBLE CHARACTERS

125 INDEX OF BIBLE REFERENCES

126 ACKNOWLEDGEMENTS

I am like a sheltered olive tree protected by the Lord himself   PSALM 52:8

INTRODUCTION

by Dave Foster

PEOPLE OF THE BOOK was born—appropriately enough—in the Jewish Quarter of Jerusalem's Old City. After a busy day, I happened to walk into the art gallery of Elyada Merioz. There, among an interesting collection of pictures, were several paintings by Jossi Stern.

For years I admired the work of this artist but had never met him. His wide range of artistic expression fascinated me. By viewing his pictures I gained an insight to the man . . . his love for Jerusalem . . . his sense of humour . . . his acute powers of observation . . . his sheer joy of living . . . and his refusal either to be bound by the restrictions of a single style or to be pushed into a stultifying mould by pressures of the *avant-garde*. I could relax and enjoy his pictures without needing to have them explained!

Working with creative people can be a traumatic experience. Some artists are notoriously temperamental. Jossi Stern is exceptional. Even under the pressure of deadlines, he is fun to work with, and exhilarating rather than exhausting. And our metabolisms match. We both thrive on late nights and a gentle, easy adjustment to the demands of a new day! And Jossi will work relentlessly for anyone who respects his daily addiction to the swimming pool of the King David Hotel!

Whether wielding a brush in his studio or eating a midnight goulash at the Jerusalem Artists' House, he is always a delight to be with, a refreshing and stimulating co-worker and companion—and a perennial philosopher.

The original idea—from which we deviated, but can still see simmering in the background for future development, was simply to illustrate the Bible. To prepare for this the artist started re-reading the Book of his people in a modern paraphrased format. This contemporary presentation brought age-old stories to life again so vividly that he would often drop the Bible, grab a litho crayon and start sketching the person about whom he was reading. When I saw the brilliant characterizations this produced, my mind started moving in new directions—and came to rest on the embryo of the idea for the present book.

It would need a much larger volume to give complete coverage to the people of the Book. I was willing to settle for less and to give the artist the freedom of choosing arbitrarily those he would portray. Inevitably some of the great characters of the Bible are missing. There are some gaps in the sequence of the story. And some events which forcibly impressed the artist may be considered by others to be relatively unimportant compared with great dramas he has chosen not to illustrate. But while this does not set out to represent the entire Biblical narrative, I believe it will stimulate others as it did us to re-read this great Book of the Jewish people which has made its impact on all mankind.

7

The creative work for such a volume was made easy by being in Jerusalem. Many of the people walking its streets today are perfect models for their Biblical forefathers. We'd see a soldier sipping coffee in the Mahane Yehuda marketplace. "There's Jonathan!" I'd exclaim.

At that point Jossi may still be sketching a man selling tomatoes. Could the facial contours of a simple street merchant be the basis for a characterization of King Solomon? I saw that with the prolific pen of this artist, anything can happen!

But while the dark-robed Rabbi was an obvious model, what part could the tee-shirted *kibbutznik* or the skimpy-skirted police girl have in PEOPLE OF THE BOOK?

Suddenly it dawned on me. While our first concept revolved around Bible characters, it is impossible to be in Israel—and particularly in Jerusalem—without recognizing the bridge across the centuries, built by such prophets as Ezekiel and Zechariah, confirming the fact that those who live and work in this capital city today are still people of the Book.

The Hebrew term *Am ha-Sefer* means not just "a people of the book" but "*the* people of *the* Book." Israeli schoolchildren study the Bible in its original language, with the added advantage of visiting sites where events recorded actually took place. Holy writ permeates every aspect of daily life in Israel . . . on radio and television, in advertising, political speeches and folk songs. The revival of Hebrew means that a language which, for centuries, was linked exclusively to prayer and piety is now the vernacular of the marketplace for Israel's polyglot people.

Today's Israeli may not relate directly to the Bible's historical passages, but he can be recognized in its prophecies. He is part of the continuing drama of the people of the Book. Prophecies which echoed down through the centuries, across the mountain-top at Masada, through the beleaguered back streets of the Warsaw ghetto, the horror of the Holocaust, and in the battle-scarred Jewish Quarter of Jerusalem's Old City in 1948 are beginning to take on fresh significance. Israel's former Foreign Minister Abba Eban once claimed: "The special pathos of Jewish history lies in the immense problem of being Jewish and yet staying alive".

With four wars of survival behind them since the establishment of the new State of Israel in 1948, the Jewish people still look forward to the time when, as Isaiah and Micah prophesied, men "will beat their swords into plowshares and their spears into pruning-hooks; nations shall no longer fight each other, for all war will end".

Then, for the people of the Book in their land of Israel and the City of David, a new day will come—on which the sun may already be rising —when, as God promises, "I will bring them home again to live safely in Jerusalem, and they will be my people, and I will be their God".

PREFACE by Jossi Stern

Many of the world's great artists have painted well-known pictures inspired by the Book of my people—the Bible. The fact that I am now turning to the same source of inspiration for this art volume is inevitable. Let me explain.

For the past thirty-five years I have lived in the same old house in Jerusalem. It has a balcony overlooking the Valley of the Cross, at the end of which is an ancient Crusader monastery. From one window I can see the hills of Beit Jala, and beyond that Bethlehem—birthplace of David and Jesus. In another direction I can see the burial place of the Prophet Samuel. Directly across the valley is the Knesset—Israel's parliament and an impressive symbol of our modern/ancient nation.

My nearest neighbour is the Rabbi Gamliel. Yemenite villagers come to visit him during the high holidays. Their picturesque traditional costumes cause them to look as if they walked straight out of the pages of the Bible.

Alongside my home is the Sha'arei Hessed (Gate of Grace) quarter. It is the area of very pious Russian and Polish Jewry distinguished by their dark, formal clothing and large fur hats. Most of their waking hours are spent in the study of holy writ.

A few minutes away is the Nahalat Ahim (Estate of the Brothers) with its colourful and happy oriental Jews. Their sounds are joyous and musical. The smells are a mingling of rich coffee and marvellous cooking!

A few more steps and I am in the middle of the amazing Mahane Yehuda (Camp of Judah) marketplace. Here mingles a fantastic conglomeration of types, shapes and sizes! All the twelve tribes, representatives of our entire Jewish family, can be found here. For an artist it is an inspiring place. A kaleidoscope of images. A palette of colour. There's an infinite variety of fruit and vegetables of every kind that the earth can yield and God's mercy can provide.

The fishmonger could well be the model for a Biblical king, but today he is the loud-voiced king of the fishmarket. The lady buying his wares, jangling with oriental jewellery, presumably from Morocco or Tunisia, could be a daughter of the Prophets. That sad-faced beggar reminds me of Job. What better models can one find for Joseph's brothers than the muscular market porters! And

. . . the loud-voiced king of the fishmarket.

. . . the amazing Mahane Yehuda marketplace.

look at that soldier and his girl-friend . . . a perfect illustration for the Song of Solomon.

This is our Jerusalem. Working, sketching, painting here for more than a quarter of a century, I cannot escape a constant recognition of the great heritage of this place and our people. It cries out from every corner of this City of David and the Prophets. These ancient stones have seen it all. They have been mute witness to great dramas, amazing miracles and terrible tragedies. I can hear the excited and happy sounds of David's conquering soldiers. I can hear the weeping of Jeremiah as the city is destroyed. Just being here brings the Book of our people to life. Truly it is a living Bible!

The sound of the shofar . . . the peal of church bells . . . the wailing Moslem call to prayer from the Mosque . . . all are reminders that this is a special place for three monotheistic religions.

Jerusalem still overwhelms and conquers me. I live in it and am inspired to create by it. In a sense I don't paint Jerusalem and its people. I paint *with* them . . . happy in my privileged role as a modest chronicler who tries to add a few lines to the beauty and glory of this great city—the eternal home of the people of the Book.

What better models can one find for Joseph's brothers than the muscular market porters!

. . . that soldier and his girl-friend . . . a perfect illustration for the Song of Solomon.

THE PROMISE

It all began with a Promise.

"God told Abram . . . 'I will cause you to become the father of a great nation . . .'"—Genesis 12:1, 2.

The Patriarchs—Abraham, Isaac and Jacob—were led by God to a "land which I shall give unto thy seed forever".

One of Jacob's sons, Joseph, through force of circumstances beyond his control, led an Israelite migration to Egypt where, eventually, they were enslaved.

Moses was God's means of deliverance for his people. After their exodus from Egypt, the Israelites spent long years of wandering in the desert before reaching their own land once again. Here they divided into twelve tribes and attempted to repossess the territories from settlers.

Their most stubborn enemy—the Philistines—seemed to be unbeatable until a boy called David became their hero, king and symbol of national unity. He made Jerusalem his capital, placing the Ark of the Law there. Later this was enshrined in a great Temple built by his son, Solomon. It sealed Jerusalem's position as the eternal capital of the Jewish people.

In 930 BCE, the kingdom divided—Israel in the North and Judah in the South. Without the strength of their previous unity, both segments were later conquered—Israel by the Assyrians (722 BCE) and Judah by the Babylonians (586 BCE). The First Temple was destroyed and the Jews exiled until 538 BCE. Solomon's Temple was then rebuilt.

Other conquerors came, such as Alexander the Great (332 BCE), the Ptolemies of Egypt and the Seleucids of Syria. Judah the Maccabee led the fight against the latter, succeeded and then re-dedicated the Temple.

Roman rule followed with the subsequent crowning of King Herod (40 BCE). During his reign, a Jew named Jesus was born and again the course of history was profoundly affected.

Rebellion against Rome broke out in 66 CE, but was crushed after the siege of Jerusalem and the destruction of the Second Temple by Titus four years later. One of the greatest stories of Jewish resistance and courage took place on a mountaintop at Masada alongside the Dead Sea. After this began the dispersion of the Jewish people throughout the world for the next 2000 years.

The short-lived Bar-Kochba rebellion (132-135 CE) failed to reclaim Jewish sovereignty over their Promised Land. Byzantine Christians came in 326 CE and established their own holy sites. They lost the land to Moslems in the year 640 until, some four-and-a-half centuries later, the Crusaders reclaimed the territory for Christianity. Islam returned to supremacy in 1291. Then came the Egyptian Mamelukes and the Ottoman Turks who, after 400 years of possession, were defeated by the British in 1917.

Pogroms, persecution and intolerance were the experience of many Jews in the lands of their dispersion. Events such as the Spanish Inquisition drove many back to the land of God's Promise to Abraham. Hopes which had never been fully extinguished were fanned into flames as Theodor Herzl founded the Zionist movement and Jews began to buy back their land, bit by precious bit. They drained the swamps, irrigated arid areas and generally made it more like a home should be.

Between 1939 and 1945, six million Jews were murdered by the Nazis in Europe. Survivors of this Holocaust and an ever-increasing number of other Jewish immigrants streamed back to the land of their forefathers. The British Mandate ended as the United Nations paved the way for the proclamation of the present State of Israel on May 14, 1948.

The people of the Book were home!

Ezekiel prophesied: "I am gathering the people of Israel from among the nations and bringing them home from around the world to their own land, to unify them into one nation"—Ezekiel 37:21, 22.

God told Abram:

"Leave your own country behind you,
and your own people,
and go to the land I will guide you to.
If you do, I will cause you to become
the father of a great nation . . ."

GENESIS 12:1, 2

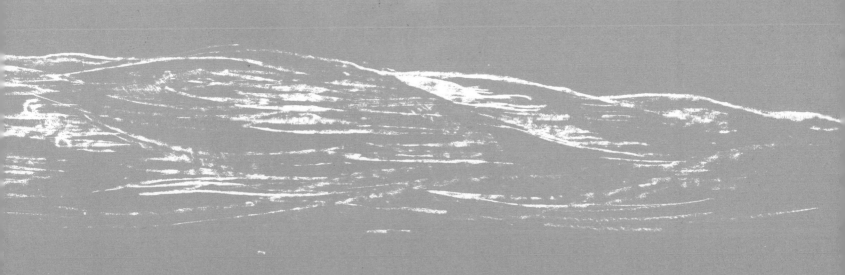

Then God brought Abram outside beneath the night-time sky and told him, "Look up into the heavens and count the stars if you can. Your descendants will be like that—too many to count." GENESIS 15:5

God's promise to Abram was endorsed by a name change.
God told him,

> *"I am changing your name. It is no longer 'Abram' ('Exalted Father'),*
> *but 'Abraham' ('Father of Nations')—for that is what you will be."*
>
> Genesis 17:5

The first ancestor of the Jewish people is also regarded as
the father of monotheism (the worship of one God),
indicated by his willingness to sacrifice the heir of God's
promise, Isaac. God's promises to Abraham related to "a
people" and "a land". The people became the channel
through which God influenced all mankind. The land
became the stage on and around which the drama of
human history has been, is and will be enacted.

*Hagar gave Abram a son, and
Abram named him Ishmael.*

GENESIS 16:15

"Isaac is the son through whom my promise will be fulfilled."

GENESIS 21:12

The succession of the first Jewish family is traced through Isaac to Jacob. God's dual promise concerning "a people" and "a land" was repeated to Jacob whose twelve children became foundation stones of the Jewish nation.

Jacob:
"Father?"
Isaac: "Yes?
Who is it, my
son—Esau or
Jacob?"
Jacob: "It's
Esau, your
oldest son."
GENESIS 27:18, 19

So Jacob . . . lay down to sleep, and dreamed that a staircase reached from earth to heaven, and he saw the angels of God going up and down upon it. At the top of the stairs stood the Lord. "I am Jehovah," he said, "the God of Abraham, and of your father Isaac. The ground you are lying on is yours! I will give it to you and to your descendants. For you will have descendants as many as dust! They will cover the land from east to west and from north to south; and all the nations of the earth will be blessed through you and your descendants. What's more, I am with you, and will protect you wherever you go, and I will bring you back safely to this land; I will be with you constantly until I have finished giving you all I am promising."

GENESIS 28:10-15

Isaac called for Jacob and blessed him and said to him, "Don't marry one of these Canaanite girls. Instead . . . marry one of your cousins—your Uncle Laban's daughters. God almighty bless you and give you many children; may you become a great nation of many tribes!"

GENESIS 28:1-3

Now Laban had two daughters, Leah, the older

. . . had lovely eyes . . .

GENESIS 29:16,17

. . . but Rachel was shapely, and in every way a beauty.

Jacob was in love with Rachel.

GENESIS 29:17,18

Joseph—the son most loved by his father Jacob—was not popular with his brothers. They plotted against him, made their father believe he was dead and pocketed the twenty pieces of silver for which they sold him into slavery.

Jacob's son Joseph was now seventeen years old . . . loved . . . more than any of his other children, because Joseph was born to him in his old age . . . His brothers . . . noticed his father's partiality, and consequently hated Joseph . . .''

GENESIS 37:2-4

Potiphar, an officer of Egypt's Pharaoh . . . captain of the palace guard . . . chief executioner . . . was Joseph's master. All was well until the young Israelite refused the advances of Potiphar's wife. Her subsequent lying and anger led to his imprisonment. But Joseph returned to become second only to Pharaoh in the land. He paved the way for his family to escape famine by coming to Egypt. There the Israelites flourished until a new Pharaoh was enthroned who felt nothing for Joseph and eventually pushed the Jews into total slavery.

Potiphar's wife began making eyes at Joseph . . .
GENESIS 39:7

THE TWELVE TRIBES

Then Jacob called together all his sons and said, "Gather around me and I will tell you what is going to happen to you in the days to come. Listen to me, O sons of Jacob; listen to Israel your father.

"Reuben, you are my oldest son, the child of my vigorous youth. You are the head of the list in rank and in honour. But you are unruly as the wild waves of the sea, and you shall be first no longer. I am demoting you, for you slept with one of my wives and thus dishonoured me.

"Simeon and Levi are two of a kind. They are men of violence and injustice. O my soul, stay away from them. May I never be a party to their wicked plans. For in their anger they murdered a man, and maimed oxen just for fun. Cursed be their anger, for it is fierce and cruel. Therefore, I will scatter their descendants throughout Israel.

"Judah, your brothers shall praise you. You shall destroy your enemies. Your father's sons shall bow before you. Judah is a young lion that has finished eating its prey. He has settled down as a lion—who will dare to rouse him? The sceptre shall not depart from Judah until Shiloh comes, whom all people shall obey. He has chained his steed to the choicest vine, and washed his clothes in wine. His eyes are darker than wine and his teeth are whiter than milk.

"Zebulun shall dwell on the shores of the sea and shall be a harbour for ships, with his borders extending to Sidon.

"Issachar is a strong beast of burden resting among the saddle bags. When he saw how good the countryside was, how pleasant the land, he willingly bent his shoulder to the task and served his masters with vigour.

"Dan shall govern his people like any other tribe in Israel. He shall be a serpent in the path that bites the horses' heels, so that the rider falls off. I trust in your salvation, Lord.

A marauding band shall stamp upon Gad, but he shall rob and pursue them!

"Asher shall produce rich foods, fit for kings!

"Naphtali is a deer let loose, producing lovely fawns.

"Joseph is a fruitful tree beside a fountain. His branches shade the wall. He has been severely injured by those who shot at him and persecuted him, but their weapons were shattered by the Mighty One of Jacob, the Shepherd, the Rock of Israel. May the God of your fathers, the Almighty, bless you with blessings of heaven above and of the earth beneath—blessings of the breasts and of the womb, blessings of the grain and flowers, blessings reaching to the utmost bounds of the everlasting hills. These shall be the blessings upon the head of Joseph who was exiled from his brothers.

"Benjamin is a wolf that prowls. He devours his enemies in the morning, and in the evening divides the spoil."

GENESIS 49:1–27

Simeon and Levi are two of a kind

SIMEON

REUBEN

Reuben . . . the child of my vigorous youth

LEVI

JUDAH

Judah . . . a young lion that has finished eating its prey

ZEBULUN

ISSACHAR

Zebulun shall dwell on the shores of the sea . . . Issachar is a strong beast of burden

32

Dan shall govern his people like any other tribe in Israel

GAD

DAN

ASHER

A marauding band shall stamp upon Gad . . Asher shall produce rich foods

33

NAPHTALI

JOSEPH

BENJAMIN

*Joseph is a fruitful tree . . . Benjamin . . . a
wolf that prowls*

34

A man named Moses . . . an Israelite . . .
raised as a prince in Egypt . . . exiled . . .
and recalled to be God's means of
deliverance for his people. He became
their leader to the Promised Land.
To Moses, on Mount Sinai, was given
the moral precepts which have become
God's plumbline for perfect living not
only for the Jewish nation but for all
mankind.

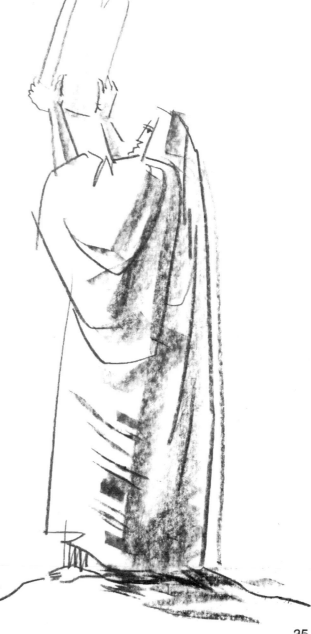

*. . . the Lord spoke to Moses face to face, as a
man speaks to his friend.*
EXODUS 33:11

A princess, one of Pharaoh's daughters, came down to bathe in the river, and as she and her maids were walking along the river bank, she spied a little boat among the reeds and sent one of the maids to bring it to her. When she opened it, there was a baby!

EXODUS 2:5,6

Moses was tending the flock of his father-in-law Jethro, the priest of Midian, out at the edge of the desert near Horeb, the mountain of God . . .

EXODUS 3:1

39

. . . suddenly the Angel of Jehovah appeared to him as a flame of fire in a bush.
When Moses saw that the bush was on fire and that it didn't burn up, he went
over to investigate. Then God called out to him,
"Moses! Moses!"
"Who is it?" Moses asked.
"Don't come any closer," God told him. "Take off your shoes, for you are
standing on holy ground. I am the God of your fathers—the God of Abraham,
Isaac and Jacob."
(Moses covered his face with his hands, for he was afraid to look at God.)
Then the Lord told him, "I have seen the deep sorrows of my people in Egypt . . .
I am going to send you to Pharaoh, to demand that he let you lead my people
out of Egypt."
"But I'm not the person for a job like that!" Moses exclaimed.
Then God told him, "I will certainly be with you, and this is the proof that I am
the one who is sending you: When you have led the people out of Egypt, you
shall worship God here upon this mountain!"

EXODUS 3:2-7, 10-12

Jehovah saved Israel . . . from the Egyptians; and the people of Israel saw the Egyptians dead, washed up on the seashore. When the people of Israel saw the mighty miracle the Lord had done for them against the Egyptians, they were afraid and revered the Lord, and believed in him and in his servant Moses.

EXODUS 14:30,31

Then Miriam the prophetess, the sister of Aaron, took a timbrel and led the women in dances. And Miriam sang this song:
> *"Sing to the Lord, for he has*
>   *triumphed gloriously.*
> *The horse and rider have been*
>   *drowned in the sea."*

EXODUS 15:20,21

. . . the people spoke bitterly against Moses and
Aaron.
"Oh, that we were back in Egypt," they
moaned, "and that the Lord had killed us there!
For we had plenty to eat. But now you have
brought us into this wilderness to kill us with
starvation."

EXODUS 16:2,3

When Moses didn't come back down the mountain right away
. . . Aaron melted the gold, then moulded and tooled it into the
form of a calf . . . So they were up early the next morning and
began offering burnt offerings and peace offerings to the
calf-idol; afterwards they sat down to feast and drink at a wild
party . . . Moses saw the calf and the dancing . . .

EXODUS 32:1,4,6,19

Conquest of the Promised Land was the part of
Moses' successor, Joshua. After forty years of
leadership through the wilderness to within
sight of the destination, the lawgiver died. The
warrior took over . . .

*Joshua (son of Nun) was full of the spirit of wisdom, for
Moses had laid his hands upon him; so the people of
Israel obeyed him . . .*
DEUTERONOMY 34:9

*"Today," the Lord told Joshua, "I will give you great honour, so that all Israel
will know that I am with you just as I was with Moses."*
JOSHUA 3:7

*. . . as the priests blew a long, loud trumpet blast, Joshua yelled to the people, "**Shout!** The Lord has given us the city!"*

JOSHUA 6:16

A long period of struggle and warfare ensued as the tribes of Israel possessed their own particular areas of the Promised Land. Some battles were unorthodox, bearing the mark of Divine intervention, as at Jericho. Others were not so spectacularly successful, as at Ai when the Israelites suffered defeat because of the disobedience of a man named Aachan . . .

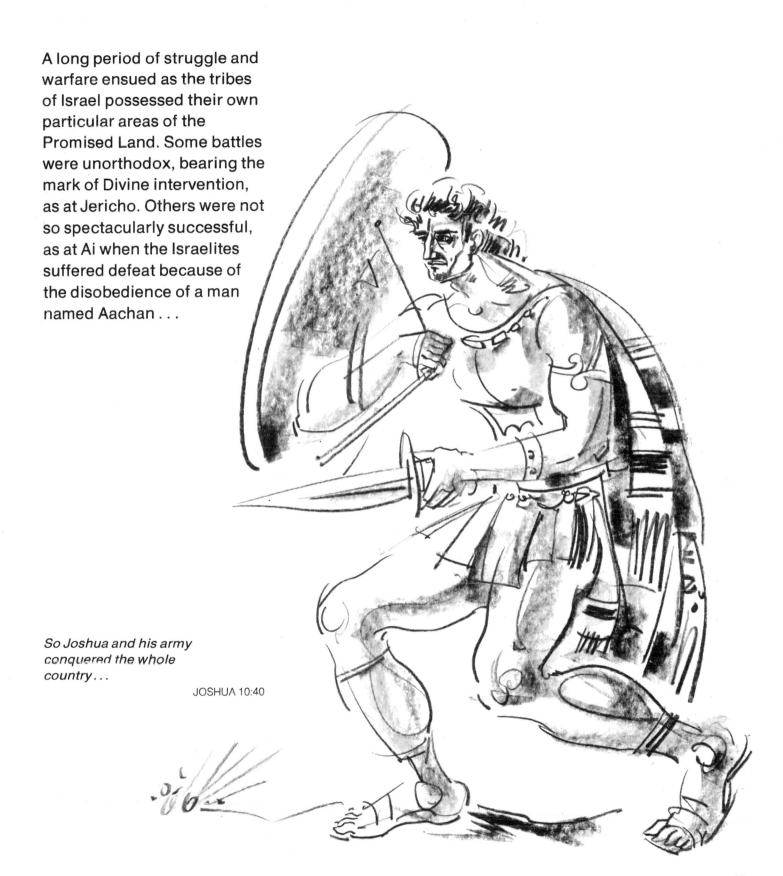

So Joshua and his army conquered the whole country . . .

JOSHUA 10:40

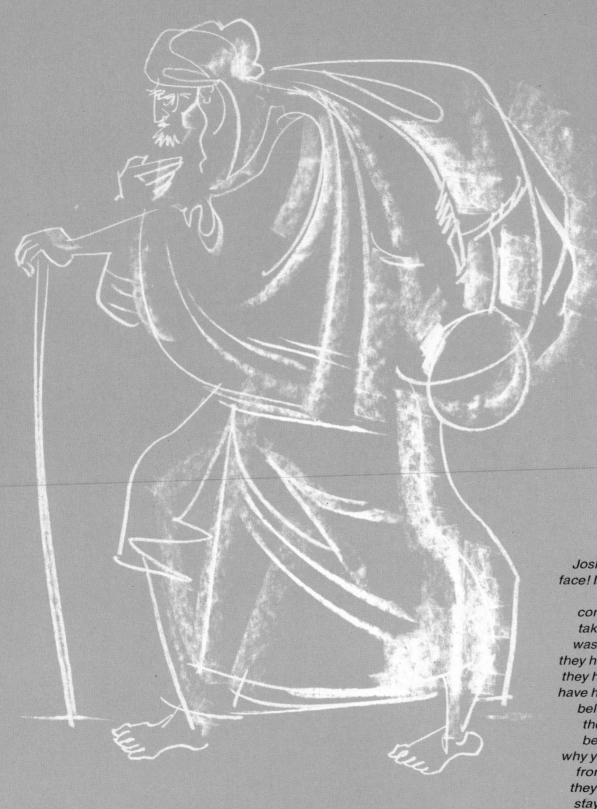

But the Lord said to Joshua, "Get up off your face! Israel has sinned and disobeyed my commandment and has taken loot when I said it was not to be taken; and they have not only taken it, they have lied about it and have hidden it among their belongings. That is why the people of Israel are being defeated. That is why your men are running from their enemies—for they are cursed. I will not stay with you any longer unless you completely rid yourselves of this sin."

JOSHUA 7:10-12

It was just after midnight and the change of guards when Gideon and the hundred men with him crept to the outer edge of the camp of Midian.

Suddenly they blew their trumpets and broke their clay jars so that their torches blazed into the night. Then the other two hundred of his men did the same, blowing the trumpets in their right hands, and holding the flaming torches in their left hands, all yelling, "For the Lord and for Gideon!"

JUDGES 7:19, 20

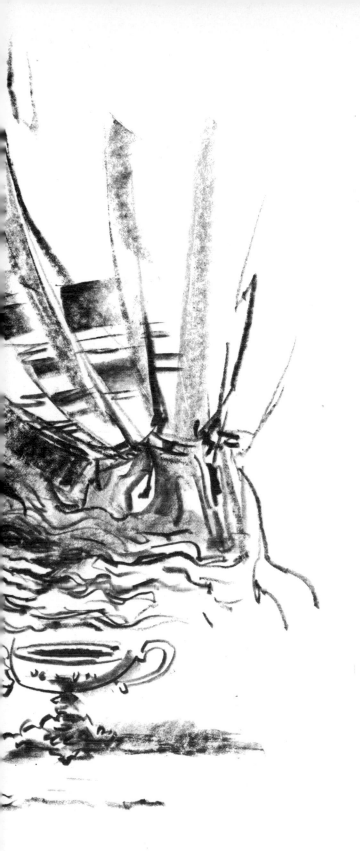

Delilah begged Samson
to tell her his secret.

JUDGES 16:6

Romance relieves the tense drama in many parts of Jewish history. The classic story of Ruth, a Moabite girl, and the wealthy landowner Boaz paves the way toward one of Israel's greatest heroes. Their son Obed was the grandfather of King David.

At lunch time Boaz called to her,
"Come and eat with us."

RUTH 2:14

Tribal rivalries often divided Israel. Foreign invaders plagued them . . . most notably, the Philistines. Samuel, the last and most distinguished of the Judges of Israel, encouraged the unity of the nation against the enemy by anointing Saul, from the tribe of Benjamin, to be the first king. Saul was not completely successful and, finally, he and his elder sons were killed in battle.

David, the son of Jesse, a farmer of the tribe of Judah, proved his prowess against the Philistines in a successful single-handed battle with their seemingly invincible champion Goliath.

He married the king's daughter and established a strong bond of friendship with the king's son, Jonathan.

David became king of his own tribe of Judah and, nearly a decade later, became the ruler of a re-united Israelite nation. His victory over the Philistines complete, he made Jerusalem the capital of his kingdom.

He was a fine looking boy, ruddy-faced, and with pleasant eyes. And the Lord said, "This is the one; anoint him."
1 SAMUEL 16:12

The Spirit of the Lord had left Saul, and

instead, the Lord had sent a tormenting spirit

that filled him with depression and fear . . . And

whenever the tormenting spirit from God

troubled Saul, David would play the harp and

Saul would feel better . . .

1 SAMUEL 16:14,23

David, the son of Jesse . . .
David, the man to whom God gave such wonderful success;
David, the anointed of the God of Jacob;
David, the sweet psalmist of Israel.

2 SAMUEL 23:1

Saul's daughter Michal had fallen in love with David, and Saul was delighted when he heard about it.

1 SAMUEL 18:20

David met Jonathan, the king's son, and

there was an immediate bond of love

between them. Jonathan swore to be his

blood brother . . .

1 SAMUEL 18:1,3

*Saul . . . instructed his aides to try to find a medium so that he could ask her
what to do, and they found one at Endor. Saul disguised himself by wearing
ordinary clothing instead of his royal robes. He went to the woman's home at
night, accompanied by two of his men.*

"I've got to talk to a dead man," he pleaded. "Will you bring his spirit up?"

*"Are you trying to get me killed?" the woman demanded. "You know that
Saul has had all of the mediums and fortune-tellers executed. You are spying
on me."*

But Saul took a solemn oath that he wouldn't betray her.

Finally the woman said, "Well, whom do you want me to bring up?"

"Bring me Samuel," Saul replied.

*When the woman saw Samuel, she screamed, "You've deceived me! You
are Saul!"*

"Don't be frightened!" the king told her. "What do you see?"

"I see a spectre coming up out of the earth," she said.

"What does he look like?"

"He is an old man wrapped in a robe."

Saul realised that it was Samuel and bowed low before him.

"Why have you disturbed me by bringing me back?" Samuel asked Saul.

*"Because I am in deep trouble," he replied. "The Philistines are at war with
us, and God has left me and won't reply by prophets or dreams; so I have
called for you to ask you what to do."*

*But Samuel replied, "Why ask me if the Lord has left you and has become
your enemy? He has done just as he said he would and has taken the
kingdom from you and given it to your rival, David. All this has come upon
you because you did not obey the Lord's instructions when he was so angry
with Amelek. What's more, the entire Israeli army will be routed and
destroyed by the Philistines tomorrow, and you and your sons will be here
with me."*

Saul now fell full length upon the ground, paralysed with fright. . . .

1 SAMUEL 28:7-20

O Israel, your pride and joy lies dead upon the hills;
Mighty heroes have fallen.
Don't tell the Philistines, lest they rejoice.
Hide it from the cities of Gath and Ashkelon,
Lest the heathen nations laugh in triumph.
O Mount Gilboa,
Let there be no dew nor rain upon you,
Let no crops of grain grow on your slopes.
For there the mighty Saul has died;
He is God's appointed king no more.
Both Saul and Jonathan slew their strongest foes,
And did not return from battle empty-handed.
How much they were loved, how wonderful they were—
Both Saul and Jonathan!
They were together in life and in death.
They were swifter than eagles, stronger than lions.
But now, O women of Israel, weep for Saul;
He enriched you
With fine clothing and golden ornaments.
These mighty heroes have fallen in the midst of the battle.
Jonathan is slain upon the hills.
How I weep for you, my brother Jonathan;
How much I loved you!
And your love for me was deeper
Than the love of women!
The mighty ones have fallen,
Stripped of their weapons, and dead.

2 SAMUEL 1:19-27

No one in Israel was such a handsome specimen of manhood as Absalom, and no one else received such praise. He cut his hair only once a year . . .

2 SAMUEL 14:25,26

Solomon is sitting on the throne and all the people are congratulating King David, saying, "May God bless you even more through Solomon than he has blessed you personally! May God make Solomon's reign even greater than yours!"

1 KINGS 1:46,47

When the Queen of Sheba heard how wonderfully the Lord had blessed Solomon with wisdom . . . she arrived in Jerusalem . . .

1 KINGS 10:1,2

My beloved is a bouquet of flowers in the gardens of En Gedi. How beautiful you are, my love, how beautiful . . . You are like a lovely orchard bearing precious fruit, with the rarest of perfumes . . .

SONG OF SOLOMON 1:14,15 & 4:13

The people experienced mixed fortunes under a
succession of kings—good, bad and indifferent.
After the reign of David's son Solomon,
the nation was again divided.
But then, amid the ebb and
flow of history was heard
the voice of the prophets.

Ahab . . . did more to anger the Lord God of Israel than any of the other kings of Israel before him.

1 KINGS 16:33

. . . he married Jezebel . . . and then began worshipping Baal.

1 KINGS 16:31

Then Elijah, the prophet from Tishbe in Gilead, told King Ahab,
"As surely as the Lord God of Israel lives—the God whom I
worship and serve—there won't be any dew or rain for several
years . . ."

1 KINGS 17:1

Elijah climbed to the top of Mount Carmel and got down on his knees . . . his servant told him, "I saw a little cloud about the size of a man's hand rising from the sea" . . . And sure enough, the sky was soon black with clouds, and a heavy wind brought a terrific rainstorm.

1 KINGS 18:42,44,45

*. . . suddenly a chariot of fire, drawn by
horses of fire, appeared . . . and Elijah
was carried by a whirlwind into heaven.*

2 KINGS 2:11

. . . for six years . . . Athaliah reigned as queen . . .
When Athaliah heard all the noise, she ran into the
Temple and saw the new king standing beside the
pillar, as was the custom at times of coronation,
surrounded by her bodyguard and many trumpeters;
and everyone was rejoicing and blowing trumpets.
"Treason! Treason!" she screamed . . .

2 KINGS 11:3,13,14

Now there was a certain Jew at the palace

named Mordecai . . .

ESTHER 2:5

This man had a beautiful and lovely young cousin, Hadassah (also called Esther), whose father and mother were dead, and whom he had adopted into his family and raised as his own daughter.

ESTHER 2:7

Vanity of Vanities
All is Vanity

I, the Preacher, was king of Israel, living in Jerusalem. And I applied my-self to search for understanding about everything in the universe . . . There is a right time for everything:

A time to be born
A time to die
A time to plant
A time to harvest
A time to kill
A time to heal
A time to destroy
A time to rebuild
A time to cry
A time to laugh
A time to grieve
A time to dance
A time for scattering stones
A time for gathering stones
A time to hug
A time not to hug
A time to find
A time to lose
A time for keeping
A time for throwing away
A time to tear
A time to repair
A time to be quiet
A time to speak up
A time for loving
A time for hating
A time for war
A time for peace

What does one really get from hard work? I have thought about this in connection with all the various kinds of work God has given to mankind. Everything is appropriate in its own time. But though God has planted eternity in the hearts of men, even so, man cannot see the whole scope of God's work from beginning to end. So I conclude that, first, there is nothing better for a man than to be happy and to enjoy himself as long as he can; and second, that he should eat and drink, and enjoy the fruits of his labours, for these are gifts from God.

And I know this, that whatever God does is final—nothing can be added or taken from it; God's purpose in this is that man should fear the all-powerful God.

ECCLESIASTES 1:12 & 3:1-14

My heart, my heart—I writhe in pain; my heart pounds within me. I cannot be still because I have heard, O my soul, the blast of the enemies' trumpets and the enemies' battle cries. Wave upon wave of destruction rolls over the land, until it lies in utter ruin; suddenly, in a moment, every house is crushed. How long must this go on? How long must I see war and death surrounding me?

JEREMIAH 4:19-21

The Prophets
of Israel...

Again and again down through the years, God has sent . . . his prophets . . .

JEREMIAH 25:4

The Prophets of Israel were God's mouthpiece to the nation. They became the conscience of the Jewish people, thundering out their messages of warning against wickedness. They came from many areas and were of widely differing backgrounds. Some were great orators while others recorded their prophetic statements in writing. Unequivocal in their condemnation of deviance from God's way, some of their prophecies provided a contrast in messages of comfort and hope. Such divinely-inspired promises came into sharp focus when the Jews were dispersed around the world and the land dispossessed. Today the voices of the Prophets ring down through the centuries with new relevance as the return to the land which they foretold is finding twentieth century fulfilment.

There lived in the land of Uz a man named Job—a good man who feared God and stayed away from evil.

JOB 1:1

Job's friends . . . were Eliphaz the Temanite,

Bildad the Shuhite and Zophar the

Naamathite.

JOB 2:11

This is another message to Isaiah from the Lord

concerning Judah and Jerusalem:

In the last days Jerusalem and the Temple of the

Lord will become the world's greatest attraction,

and people from many lands will flow there to

worship the Lord.

"Come," everyone will say, "let us go up the

mountain of the Lord, to the Temple of the God of

Israel; there he will teach us his laws, and we will

obey them." For in those days the world will be

ruled from Jerusalem. The Lord will settle

international disputes; all the nations will convert

their weapons of war into implements of peace.

ISAIAH 2:1-4

The Lord their God will save his people . . . as a Shepherd caring for his sheep. They shall shine in his land as glittering jewels in a crown.

ZECHARIAH 9:16,17

Amos was a herdsman living in the village of Tekoa . . . One day, in a vision, God told him some of the things that were going to happen to his nation, Israel.

AMOS 1:1,2

God has told you what he wants, and this is all it is: to be fair and just and merciful, and to walk humbly with your God.

MICAH 6:8

*I will refresh Israel like
the dew from heaven . . .
Her people will return
from exile far away . . .*
HOSEA 14:5, 7

This message came to Jeremiah from the Lord at the beginning of the reign of Jehoiakim (son of Josiah), king of Judah: Make a yoke and fasten it on your neck . . .

JEREMIAH 27:1,2

The power of the Lord was upon me and I was carrled away by the Spirit of the Lord to a valley full of old, dry bones . . .

"These bones," he said, "represent all the people of Israel. They say: 'We have become a heap of dried-out bones—all hope is gone.' But tell them, the Lord God says: My people, I will open your graves of exile . . .

EZEKIEL 37:1,2,11,12

. . . and cause you to rise again
and return to the land of Israel.
And, then at last, O my people,
you will know I am the Lord.

EZEKIEL 37:12,13

101

I will rebuild the City of David . . . and return it to its former glory . . .

AMOS 9:11

O Israel, you are mine, my chosen ones; for you are Abraham's family, and he was my friend.   ISAIAH 41:8

104

I will firmly plant them there upon the land that I have given them . . .

AMOS 9:15

O mountains of Israel, again you will be filled with homes . . . My people will walk upon you once again, and you will belong to them again . . .

EZEKIEL 36:11,12

I will open up rivers for them on high plateaus! I will give them fountains of water in the valleys! In the deserts will be pools of water, and rivers fed by springs shall flow across the dry, parched ground. I will plant trees . . . on barren land.

ISAIAH 41:18,19

Acreage will be cultivated again that through the years of exile lay empty as a barren wilderness; all who passed by were shocked to see the extent of ruin in your land. But when I bring you back they will say, 'This God-forsaken land has become like Eden's garden!'

EZEKIEL 36:34,35

"I will restore the fortunes of my people Israel, and they shall rebuild their ruined cities, and live in them again, and they shall plant vineyards and gardens and eat their crops and drink their wine."

AMOS 9:14

Just as the mountains
surround and protect Jerusalem,
so the Lord
surrounds and protects his people.

PSALM 125:2

O Jerusalem, may there be peace within your walls . . .

PSALM 122:7

For the Lord God says: I am gathering the people of Israel from among the nations, and bringing them home from around the world to their own land, to unify them into one nation.

EZEKIEL 37:21,22

CITY OF THE BOOK

by Teddy Kollek
Mayor of Jerusalem

If Jews are the People of the Book, then Jerusalem is the City of the Book. Since King David made this ancient city his capital, nearly three thousand years ago, the attachment of the Jewish people to Jerusalem has remained constant. The perennial prayer of the Jew was for a return to Jerusalem and this bond was a significant factor in the rebirth of the State of Israel. It is enshrined in our national anthem:

To live in freedom in the Land
Of Zion and Jerusalem.

The physical association of the Jewish people with their holy city has been interrupted by a succession of intruders, but broken only three times. In the year 135, Hadrian drove all Jews out of the city and destroyed it. In 1099, there was the total annihilation of both Moslems and Jews by the Crusaders. Then, in 1948, the Jewish Quarter of the Old City fell to invading Arab forces and, for the third time, Jews were driven out. For the next nineteen years the city was divided.

It was not until the Six Day War of 1967 that heavy shelling by the Jordanians led to Israeli retaliation. This resulted in the liberation of the Jewish Quarter and the reunification of the entire city.

On being elected Mayor of Jerusalem at the end of 1965, I dreamed that the city would one day be reunited, but had no idea it would happen so soon and so dramatically. Now, for more than a decade, I have had the privilege (and pressures!) of presiding over this dynamic and developing city, seeing those who regard it as sacred—whether Jew, Moslem or Christian—free to follow their faith and worship God in their own distinctive way. But for its oldest inhabitants, the People of the Book, it is the answer to the prayer of two thousand years.

In his introduction, Dave Foster refers to the fact that the idea of this book was conceived in the Jewish Quarter of the Old City. The location is appropriate because the tragedy and triumph of this 20 acre area is symbolic of the people to whom it belongs. Battered, beleaguered, beaten and almost destroyed, it is now being restored. Its renewal reflects the re-establishment of the Jews in the City of David.

Jossi Stern's characterization of the patriarchs and prophets is striking, and his portrayal of present-day People of the Book and the City of the Book is most realistic. Prophetic quotations from the Bible indicate its contemporary quality. Did God have our present building projects in mind when he directed Amos to write: "I will rebuild the City of David and return it to its former glory . . ." *(Amos 9, v.11)*? Our housing shortage and building development seem to have been foreseen by Zechariah when he claimed: "Jerusalem will some day be so full of people that she won't have enough room for all! Many will live outside the city walls . . ." *(Zechariah 2, v.4)*. And perhaps the prophet had some foreknowledge of our tourist boom when he wrote: "People from around the world will come on pilgrimages and pour into Jerusalem from many foreign cities . . ." *(Zechariah 8, v.20)*!

History endorses the durability of both the Jews and Jerusalem. Prophecy predicts our future is to be even greater than our past. And, as this city is a focal point of world attention, it is reassuring to remember that God promised King David "that his dynasty will go on forever, and his throne (Jerusalem) will continue to the end of time." *(Psalm 89, vv.35, 36.)*

Jerusalem is the heart and soul of the Jewish people. If you want a single word to symbolize the history of the People of the Book, that word is Jerusalem.

Teddy Kollek

Pray for the peace of Jerusalem. May all who love

this city prosper. O Jerusalem, may there be

peace within your walls and prosperity in your

palaces.

PSALM 122:6,7

Jerusalem will some day be so full of people that she won't have room for all! Many will live outside the city walls . . .

ZECHARIAH 2:4

People from around the world will come on pilgrimages and pour into Jerusalem from many foreign cities . . .

ZECHARIAH 8:20

Jerusalem will have peace and prosperity so long that there will once again be aged men and women hobbling through her streets on canes, and the streets will be filled with children.

ZECHARIAH 8:4, 5

You can be sure that I will rescue my people from east and west, wherever they are scattered. I will bring them home again to live safely in Jerusalem, and they will be my people, and I will be their God . . .

ZECHARIAH 8:7,8

Jossi Stern

Jossi (Joseph) Stern was born in 1923 in the village of Kayar in Hungary's Bakon mountains. At the age of ten he moved to Budapest where he lived with an uncle for the next six years. As Hitler began to assemble his Nazi army and started moving east immediately before the outbreak of World War II, Jossi joined a group of young people heading for the then British-administered Palestine.

Their small ship, appropriately named after the Prophet Zechariah, finally completed its hazardous journey early in 1940. Those aboard were immediately arrested as illegal immigrants and spent the next six months in a prison camp near Haifa.

After being released, Jossi Stern was taken under the wing of the Betar Youth Aliyah. He worked in various jobs from agriculture to road building, before some friends saw his artistic potential and he was given the opportunity of studying in the prestigious Bezalel School of Arts and Crafts in Jerusalem.

After three years, he graduated and received the Hermann Struck Award as Outstanding Student. This preceded a long association with the school as an instructor in Elements of Graphic Art and in Illustration. Many of today's leading artists in Israel were once his students.

In 1947 he began a period working as an illustrator for a number of books, and had his first one-man exhibition in Yonas Gallery, Jerusalem. In the same year he had a similar exhibition at Tel Aviv's Mikra studio gallery.

A grant from the Israeli Ministry of Education in 1949 enabled him to study for a year at London's Royal College of Art under John Minton. This was followed by a year painting and studying in Paris. He returned to Jerusalem in 1951.

One-man exhibitions, the publication of water colour and pen-and-ink sketches, and contributions to a number of daily and weekly newspapers combined to make his name a household word in Israel. He made regular tours of Europe's art centres in France, Holland, Italy and Greece, and was exhibiting extensively throughout the United States and Canada.

In 1965, the Israeli Publishing Institute published a volume of his sketches and drawings. The following year he was awarded a UNESCO grant to study for one year in the United States. In 1968 he received the Laureate of Nordean Prize, and in 1970 had a one-man exhibition in London.

During the present decade, he has spent most of his time in Israel. Exhibitions in Jerusalem, Tel Aviv and Eilat have been interspersed with similar one-man shows in some of the country's culture-starved outposts—including Sinai's Abu Rudeis oilfield encampment just before it was returned to Egypt.

"The Drawings of Jossi Stern" was published in the United States in 1974. It was part of the Master Draughtsman Series which included the drawings of such artists as Da Vinci, Van Gogh, Rembrandt, Renoir, Matisse, Picasso, Dali, Goya, Lautrec and others. In fact, he was privileged to be the only Israeli artist included in this series.

Today he makes his home in Jerusalem where his original works and lithographs are in great demand at the Old City Art Gallery, inside the Zion Gate. When Egyptian President Anwar Sadat made his unprecedented trip to Jerusalem in November 1977, his Israeli hosts presented him with an oil painting, "Angel of Peace", by Jossi Stern.

Index to Bible Characters

A

Abraham 14, 16
Absalom 68
Achan 50
Ahab 74, 76, 77
Amos 93
Asher 33
Athaliah 79

B

Benjamin 34
Bildad 89
Boaz 54, 55

D

Dan 33
David 57, 59, 60
Delilah 52, 53

E

Elijah 76, 77, 78
Eliphaz 89
Esther 81
Ezekiel 98

G

Gad 33
Gideon 51

H

Hagar 18
Hosea 95

I

Isaac 19, 21
Isaiah 90
Ishmael 18
Issachar 32

J

Jacob 22
Jeremiah 84, 97
Jezebel 75
Job 88
Jonathan 62, 67
Joseph 27, 29, 34
Joshua 47
Judah 32

L

Laban 23
Leah 23, 24
Levi 31

M

Micah 94
Michal 61
Miriam 43
Mordecai 80
Moses 35, 36, 39, 41

N

Naphtali 34

P

Potiphar, Wife of 29

R

Rachel 23, 25
Reuben 31
Ruth 55

S

Samson 52, 53
Samuel 57, 65
Saul 59, 65, 67
Sheba, Queen of 70
Simeon 31
Solomon 69, 70

Z

Zebulun 32
Zechariah 92
Zophar 89

Index to Bible References

Book	Reference	Page		Book	Reference	Page
GENESIS	12:1,2	14			16:33	74
	15:5	16			17:1	76
	16:15	18			18:42,44,45	77
	21:12	19		2 KINGS	2:11	78
	27:18,19	21			11:3,13,14	79
	28:1-3	23		ESTHER	2:5	80
	28:10-15	22			2:7	81
	29:16,17	24		JOB	1:1	88
	29:17,18	25			2:11	89
	37:2-4	26		PSALMS	52:8	6
	39:7	28			122:7	111
	49:1-27	30			125:2	110
EXODUS	2:5,6	37		ECCLESIASTES	1:12	83
	3:1	38			3:1-14	83
	3:2-7,10-12	40		SONG OF		
	14:30,31	42		SOLOMON	1:14,15	71
	15:20,21	42			4:13	71
	16:2,3	44		ISAIAH	2:1-4	91
	32:1,4,6,19	45			41:8	103
	33:11	35			41:18,19	107
DEUTERONOMY	34:9	46		JEREMIAH	4:19-21	85
JOSHUA	3:7	46			25:4	87
	6:16	48			27:1,2	96
	7:10-12	50		EZEKIEL	36:11,12	106
	10:40	49			36:34,35	108
JUDGES	7:19, 20	51			37:1,2,11,12	99
	16:6	53			37:12,13	100
RUTH	2:14	54			37:21,22	112
1 SAMUEL	16:12	56		HOSEA	1:10,11	104
	16:14,23	58			14:5,7	95
	18:1,3	63		AMOS	1:1,2	93
	18:20	61			9:11	102
	28:7-20	64			9:14	109
2 SAMUEL	1:19-27	66			9:15	105
	14:25,26	68		MICAH	6:8	94
	23:1	60		ZECHARIAH	2:4	116
1 KINGS	1:46,47	69			8:4,5	118
	10:1,2	70			8:7,8	120
	16:31	75			8:20	117

ACKNOWLEDGEMENTS

We wish to place on record our sincere gratitude to the people who helped us in so many ways toward the completion of this book.

Elyada Merioz was serving us coffee in his Art Gallery when the idea was born. He gave not only encouragement but also total access to his large Jossi Stern collection for whatever we wished to use. While the vast majority of material for this volume is new and specially prepared, a few of the pictures were graciously loaned by him. His wife, Jenny, contributed helpful manuscript advice and gracious hospitality.

Jerusalem's Mayor, Teddy Kollek, took time from his hectic schedule to identify with us. His staff member, Daphna Avnon, of Jerusalem International Book Fair fame, was much more than a first-rate liaison person.

Lars Dunberg's "gamble" to get things started, and his company INTERSKRIFT'S co-operation with so many excellent co-edition publishers have resulted in PEOPLE OF THE BOOK growing to be "bigger than both of us"! Special mention should be made of Lady Collins whose enthusiasm for the project inspired us to even greater peaks of achievement!

Our thanks to the great production team, headed by Angus Hudson, his colleague Rodney Shepherd and their assistants Ann Rumsey and Carole Gardner of the British Printing Corporation, along with those at Purnells who did all the technical work.

Since most of the captions are Biblical, we are grateful to the publishers of THE LIVING BIBLE for giving us such eminently readable and easily-understood material with which to work.

To Jean Morgan, who typed the text, and to technical, theological and historical advisors too numerous to mention individually, a special *toda raba*.

—Jossi Stern & Dave Foster